Prayers for All Occasions

Prayers for All Occasions

Revised 2007

FORWARD MOVEMENT
CINCINNATI, OHIO

Nineteenth Printing
Printed in Canada

 FORWARD MOVEMENT
300 West Fourth Street
Cincinnati, Ohio 45202-2666

800-543-1813

www.forwardmovement.org

Contents

Plan for Morning Devotions

The reading of a passage from the Bible, perhaps with the daily meditation in Forward Day by Day, *should always form part of morning or evening devotions.*

1. Hold your mind for a few seconds in silent recollection of the presence of God, saying slowly: *O God, you are present in every place, help me realize your presence here and now.*

2. Say an act of praise and adoration. See pages 5-6.

3. Pray for spiritual strength and guidance for the day, followed by dedication to the doing of God's will, and an affirmation of sincere intention. See pages 7-13.

4. Say a brief intercession for family and friends, and for anyone seriously sick or bereaved.

5. Pray The Lord's Prayer.

6. Slowly repeat a short passage of scripture such as: *In quietness and in trust shall be your strength* (Isaiah 30:15) or *I am not alone, because the Father is with me* (John 16:32).

Plan for Evening Devotions

The reading of a passage from the Bible, perhaps with the daily meditation in Forward Day by Day, *should always form part of morning or evening devotions.*

1. Hold your mind for a few seconds in silent recollection of the presence of God, saying slowly: *O God, you are present in every place, help me realize your presence here and now.*

2. Say an act of thanksgiving. See pages 21-28.

3. Confess your sins, with specific mention of known sins, and pray for forgiveness, See page 41.

4. Say intercessions. More time should be given to this than in the morning, and a scheme of intercessions might be arranged for a week, such as the one suggested on pages 73-74. The mission of the church should have a place in every Christian's prayers.

5. Pray The Lord's Prayer and the *Gloria Patri.*

Acts of Praise and Adoration

Glory to God in the highest, and peace to
his people on earth.
We worship you, we give you thanks, we
praise you for your glory.

✦

Blessed are you, O Lord God of our fathers;
praised and exalted above all for ever.

✦

Glory to you, Lord God of our fathers;
you are worthy of praise; glory to you.

✦

Holy, holy, holy Lord,
God of power and might,
heaven and earth are full of your glory.

✦

We praise you, O God;
we acknowledge you to be the Lord...
And we worship your Name for ever,
world without end.

You are God: we praise you;
You are the Lord: we acclaim you...
We praise your Name for ever.

＊

Bless the Lord, O my soul; and all that is
within me, bless his holy Name.

＊

Blessed are you, O God, who has given us
the light of the knowledge of your glory
in the face of Jesus Christ.

＊

Glory to the Father, and to the Son,
and to the Holy Spirit:
As it was in the beginning, is now,
and will be for ever. Amen.

Affirmations of
Faith and Sincere Intention

The Apostles' Creed

I believe in God, the Father Almighty,
   creator of heaven and earth.
I believe in Jesus Christ, his only Son,
                  our Lord.
   He was conceived by the power of the
         Holy Spirit
   and born of the Virgin Mary.
   He suffered under Pontius Pilate,
            was crucified, died,
            and was buried.
   He descended to the dead.
   On the third day he rose again.
   He ascended into heaven,
            and is seated at the
            right hand of the Father.
   He will come again to judge
            the living and the dead.
I believe in the Holy Spirit,
   the holy catholic Church,

the communion of saints,
the forgiveness of sins,
the resurrection of the body,
and the life everlasting. Amen.

Psalm 23
(King James Version)

The Lord is my shepherd;
    I shall not want.
He maketh me to lie down in green pastures;
    he leadeth me beside the still waters.
He restoreth my soul;
    he leadeth me in the paths of
                righteousness for his
                Name's sake.
Yea, though I walk through the valley
           of the shadow of death,
I will fear no evil;
    for thou art with me;
      thy rod and thy staff they comfort me.
Thou preparest a table before me in the
           presence of mine enemies;

thou anointest my head with oil;
my cup runneth over.
Surely goodness and mercy shall follow me
all the days of my life;
and I will dwell in the house of the
Lord for ever.

Affirmations

Heavenly Father, you have made me your own, and I rejoice in the knowledge of your love through Jesus Christ our Lord. I would live this day in love of you and in obedience to your holy will. Give me your enabling grace.

Lord Jesus, I pledge to be your faithful soldier and servant to my life's end. In your abiding presence is my strength; with you as my constant companion I am fortified to meet the trials and temptations of the day.

As I abide in Christ I am supplied with all the spiritual resources for my needs.

As I abide in Christ I am free from fear and am quiet and confident within.

As I abide in Christ I am at one with God and know the peace of God which passes understanding.

I can do all things through Christ who strengthens me.

I believe I have received not the spirit of fearfulness, but of power and of love and of a sound mind.

The Lord is my keeper.

I believe in the Son of God; therefore I am in him, having redemption through his blood and life by his Spirit.

He is in me and all fullness is in him.

To him I belong by creation, purchase, conquest, and self-surrender: to me he belongs for all my hourly needs.

There is no difficulty, inward or outward, which he is not ready to meet in me today.

St. Patrick's Breastplate

I bind unto myself today
the strong Name of the Trinity,
by invocation of the same,
the Three in One and One in Three.

I bind this day to me for ever,
by power of faith, Christ's Incarnation;
his baptism in the Jordan river;
his death on cross for my salvation;
his bursting from the spicèd tomb;
his riding up the heavenly way;

his coming at the day of doom:
I bind unto myself today.

I bind unto myself the power
of the great love of cherubim;
the sweet "Well done" in judgment hour;
the service of the seraphim;
confessors' faith, apostles' word,
the patriarchs' prayers, the prophets' scrolls;
all good deeds done unto the Lord,
and purity of virgin souls.

I bind unto myself today
the virtues of the starlit heaven,
the glorious sun's life-giving ray,
the whiteness of the moon at even,
the flashing of the lightning free,
the whirling wind's tempestuous shocks,
the stable earth, the deep salt sea,
around the old eternal rocks.

I bind unto myself today
the power of God to hold and lead,
his eye to watch, his might to stay,
his ear to hearken to my need;

the wisdom of my God to teach,
his hand to guide, his shield to ward;
the word of God to give me speech,
his heavenly host to be my guard.

Christ be with me, Christ within me,
Christ behind me, Christ before me,
Christ beside me, Christ to win me,
Christ to comfort and restore me.
Christ beneath me, Christ above me,
Christ in quiet, Christ in danger,
Christ in hearts of all that love me,
Christ in mouth of friend and stranger.

I bind unto myself the Name,
the strong Name of the Trinity,
by invocation of the same,
the Three in One and One in Three.
Of whom all nature hath creation,
eternal Father, Spirit, Word:
praise to the Lord of my salvation,
salvation is of Christ the Lord.

—attributed to St. Patrick;
this text by Cecil F. Alexander, 1889

Veni Creator Spiritus

Come, Holy Ghost, our souls inspire,
and lighten with celestial fire.
Thou the anointing Spirit art,
who dost thy sevenfold gifts impart.

Teach us to know the Father, Son,
and thee, of both, to be but One,
that through the ages all along,
this may be our endless song:

Praise to thy eternal merit,
Father, Son, and Holy Spirit.

Come with us, O blessèd Jesus,
with us evermore to be;
and in leaving now thine altar,
let us nevermore leave thee!
O let thine angel chorus
cease not the heavenly strain,
but in us, thy loving children,
bring peace, good will to men.

—*John Henry Hopkins*

Daily Prayers

A Morning Prayer

I thank you, O God, for keeping me through the night, and for the promise of this new day. I would begin it with you, and pray that it may be to me a day of growth in the Spirit and of service for you and your kingdom in the world. Help me to meet with quiet confidence whatever trials the day holds for me; strengthen me against temptation; and keep me always loyal to our Lord and Savior Jesus Christ.

A Morning Resolve

I will try this day to live a simple, sincere, and serene life, repelling promptly every thought of discontent, anxiety, discouragement, impurity, and self-seeking; cultivating cheerfulness, magnanimity, charity, and the habit of holy silence; exercising economy in expenditure, generosity in giving, carefulness in conversation, diligence in appointed service, fidelity to every trust, and a childlike faith in God.

In particular I will try to be faithful in those habits of prayer, work, study, physical exercise, eating, and sleep which I believe the Holy Spirit has shown me to be right.

And as I cannot in my own strength do this, nor even with a hope of success attempt it, I look to thee, O Lord God my Father, in Jesus my Savior, and ask for the gift of the Holy Spirit.

Noon

Blessed Savior, who at this hour hung upon the cross stretching forth your loving arms, grant that all may look to you and be saved.

Almighty Savior, at noonday you called your servant Saint Paul to be an apostle to the Gentiles: We pray you to illumine the world with the radiance of your glory, that all nations may come and worship you, for you live and reign with the Father and the Holy Spirit, one God, world without end.

Give peace for all time, O Lord, and fill my heart and the hearts of all people everywhere with the Spirit of our Lord Jesus Christ.

Night

Our Father, the day is over and I turn to you before I take my rest. You have been with me all the day long, and for all your mercies, perceived and unperceived, I give thanks. Of all that has been amiss in me, in thought, word, and deed, I repent, and ask your gracious forgiveness as I also forgive all who have offended me. Grant me now the blessings of a quiet mind and a trustful spirit, the freedom from fear of a child in its father's house. So let me rest in you, at peace with you and with all people.

Guide us waking, O Lord, and guard us sleeping; that awake we may watch with Christ, and asleep we may rest in peace.

I lie down in peace; at once I fall asleep; for only you, LORD, make me dwell in safety.

— *Psalm 4:8*

A

LORD, you are in the midst of us, and we are called by your name: Do not forsake us, O LORD our God.

— *Jeremiah 14:9, 22*

A

O Lord, support us all the day long, until the shadows lengthen, and the evening comes, and the busy world is hushed, and the fever of life is over, and our work is done. Then in your mercy, grant us a safe lodging, and a holy rest, and peace at the last.

—*John Henry Newman*

Acts of
Thanksgiving

Thanksgivings

We praise you, O God, with gladness and humility for all the joys of life, for health and strength, for the love of friends, for work to do and play to recreate us. We thank you for the adventure of life. Above all, we thank you for your gift of Jesus Christ our Lord, for the blessings that have come to us through his body the church. Help us to show our thankfulness, not only with our lips, but in our lives, always endeavoring to do what shall please you.

O God, the giver of all good gifts, we thank you for all the blessings we have. Give us always contented minds, cheerful hearts, and ready wills, so that we may spend and be spent in the service of others, after the example of him who gave his life as a ransom for many, our Lord and Master, Jesus Christ.

We give thanks to you, O Father, for the holy Name which you have made to dwell in our hearts; and for the knowledge, faith, and immortality, which you have given to us through Jesus your Son. To you be glory forever.

∗

Accept, O Lord, our thanks and praise for all that you have done for us. We thank you for the splendor of the whole creation, for the beauty of this world, for the wonder of life, and for the mystery of love.

We thank you for the blessing of family and friends, and for the loving care which surrounds us on every side.

We thank you for setting us at tasks which demand our best efforts, and for leading us to accomplishments which satisfy and delight us.

We thank you also for those disappointments and failures that lead us to acknowledge our dependence on you alone.

Above all, we thank you for your Son Jesus Christ; for the truth of his Word and the example of his life; for his steadfast obedience, by which he overcame temptation; for his dying, through which he overcame death; and for his rising to life again, in which we are raised to the life of your kingdom.

Grant us the gift of your Spirit, that we may know Christ and make him known; and through him, at all times and in all places, may give thanks to you in all things. Amen.

You, Lord Almighty, have created all things for your Name's sake, and given food and drink to all people for their enjoyment, that they might give thanks to you; and on us you have bestowed spiritual food and drink, and eternal life through your Son. To you be glory forever. Remember, O Lord, your church. Deliver it from all evil and perfect it in your love. Sanctify it and gather it together into your Kingdom which you have prepared for it. For yours is the power and the glory for ever and ever.

The General Thanksgiving

Almighty God, Father of all mercies,
we thine unworthy servants
do give thee most humble and hearty thanks
for all thy goodness and loving-kindness
to us and to all men.

We bless thee for our creation, preservation,
and all the blessings of this life;
but above all for thine inestimable love
in the redemption of the world by our
Lord Jesus Christ,
for the means of grace, and for the
hope of glory.

And, we beseech thee,
give us that due sense of all thy mercies,
that our hearts may be unfeignedly thankful;
and that we show forth thy praise,
not only with our lips, but in our lives,
by giving up our selves to thy service,
and by walking before thee
in holiness and righteousness all our days;
through Jesus Christ our Lord,
to whom, with thee and the Holy Ghost,
be all honor and glory, world without end.
Amen.

Thanksgiving for Missions

O God, you have made of one blood all the nations dwelling on the face of the whole earth: We give you most humble and hearty thanks for the revelation of yourself in your Son Jesus Christ, for the commission to your church to proclaim the gospel to every creature, for those who have gone to the ends of the earth to bring light to them that dwell in darkness and in the shadow of death, and for the innumerable company who now praise your name out of every kindred and nation and tongue. To you be ascribed the praise of their faith for ever and ever.

Psalm 103:1-4

Bless the LORD, O my soul,
 and all that is within me,
   bless his holy Name.
Bless the LORD, O my soul,
 and forget not all his benefits.
He forgives all your sins
 and heals all your infirmities;

He redeems your life from the grave
and crowns you with mercy and
loving-kindness.

Psalm 146:1

I will praise the LORD, as long as I live;
I will sing praises to my God
while I have my being.

For Great and Simple Joys

We praise and thank you, Lord, for great and simple joys: For the gift of wonder, the joy of discovery, and the everlasting freshness of experience; for all that comes to us through sympathy and through sorrow; for the joy of work achieved and work not achieved from which we have learned much; for musicians, poets, artists, all who work in form and color to enhance the beauty of life; for the likeness of Christ in ordinary people, their forbearance, courage, and kindness; and for quiet and faithful service cheerfully given. For these blessings, we thank you, Lord.

Family Prayers

For the Family

Heavenly Father, we thank you for your mercies which are new every morning: For health and strength, for this day with its fresh opportunities for work and service. Bless each one of us, and hold us together in your love and in love of you. We pray for your help and guidance as we face the duties to be done, the decisions to be made, the temptations that may beset us, the disappointments that may await us. Guide us, strengthen us, keep us; and grant that in all things we may act worthily of our Christian calling.

Heavenly Father, in you we live and move and have our being: We humbly pray you so to guide and govern us by your Holy Spirit, that in all the cares and occupations of our daily life we may not forget you, but may remember that we are ever walking in your sight.

For Parents and Caregivers

Heavenly Father, from whose care we learn our pattern of parenthood, give to those who have the care of children the spirit of wisdom, patience, and love, so that the homes in which they grow up may be to them an image of your kingdom, and the care of their parents a likeness of your love.

For Children

O Lord Jesus Christ, you took children into your arms and blessed them: We pray you to keep our children ever enfolded by your love. Help them to grow in love of you; save them from evil; strengthen them against the impulse of self-will; inspire in them a high sense of truth and of the duty of human service; and give them grace to follow day by day in the steps of your most holy life.

Prayers for a Little Child

Dear Father in heaven, I thank you for Jesus, who came to bring us your love and to teach us to love one another. Help me to love everybody and to do what he would have me to do.

Dear God, I thank you for all good things: for my home, for food and clothing, for my friends, for the flowers and trees and birds—and everything. Help me to share all my good things with others.

A Boy's or Girl's Prayer

Heavenly Father, I thank you for my father and mother and for our home. Bless us all, and help us to love you, and in love to serve one another as Jesus taught us to do. Give me strength to do what is right today, and to do unto others as I would have them do unto me.

For a Birthday

Watch over your child, O Lord, as *his* days increase; bless and guide *him* wherever *he* may be. Strengthen *him* when *he* stands; comfort *him* when discouraged or sorrowful; raise *him* up if *he* falls; and in *his* heart may your peace which passes understanding abide all the days of *his* life; through Jesus Christ our Lord.

O God, our times are in your hand: Look with favor, we pray, on your servant _____ as *he* begins another year. Grant that *he* may grow in wisdom and grace, and strengthen *his* trust in your goodness all the days of *his* life; through Jesus Christ our Lord.

Grace Before Meals

Bless, O Lord, this food to our use and us to your service, and keep us ever responsive to the needs of others; for Christ's sake.

For these and all his mercies, God's holy Name be praised.

Blessed be the Lord daily for all his mercies; through Jesus Christ our Lord.

We thank you, Lord, for our daily bread both for body and soul. Keep us ever mindful of your good providence.

We give thanks to you, Almighty God, for these your earthly gifts. As our bodies are strengthened and refreshed, so may we be made strong in our souls to glorify you in our lives.

⚜

Bless and praise the Lord for his goodness.
The Lord be blessed and praised.

⚜

Thanks be to God to whom our thanks are due.
Thanks be to God for ever and ever.

Personal
Prayers

For Forgiveness

O Almighty Father, Lord of heaven and earth, I confess that I have sinned against you in thought, word, and deed. Have mercy upon me, O God, after your great goodness; according to the multitude of your mercies, do away with my offenses and cleanse me from my sins.

⚜

Almighty God, I have sinned against you, and in penitence pray for your forgiveness. In your mercy hear me, and give me strength to overcome my weakness and to live day by day according to your holy will.

⚜

Lord, I have sinned against my neighbor, and therefore also against you. Forgive me, and grant me the humility and the courage to go and admit my fault and seek reconciliation, as our Master taught us to do.

For Purity of Heart

Almighty God, to you all hearts are open, all desires known, and from you no secrets are hid: Cleanse the thoughts of my heart by the inspiration of your Holy Spirit, that I may perfectly love you, and worthily magnify your holy Name.

On Going to Work

Lord, be with me as I go to my work today. Help me to be faithful in the discharge of my duties and honorable in all my dealings. Give me self-control in speech and temper, and let me be a good example to others of Christian humility and thoughtfulness, that I may glorify you.

For Those Whose Work Is in the Home

Lord Jesus, born of Mary, help me to do all I have to do today for you. Let my task be eased by the knowledge of your presence, and of your loving care for your own. Give me a desire to do all things for love of you, strength to meet without complaint the trials of the day, and a thankful heart for all God's mercies.

For a Child Going to School

Dear God, come with me to school and be with me in my lessons and in my play. Help me to be friendly and thoughtful of others, obedient to my teachers, careful in my studies, and like Jesus in my words and deeds.

For Youth in School and College

Lord Jesus, who as a young adult heard and obeyed the call to give your life in sacrifice for the salvation of all people and for the kingdom of God: Help me in this time of my youth to discover how best to serve God. In my days of preparation at school, keep ever before my eyes the prize that is better than any earthly prize. Save me from material aims and ambitions, and direct me in all my studies that they may serve above all things to make me better prepared to do the work which you will give me to do. Keep me day by day loyal to you; strengthen me to resist the temptations of the body and the mind; and help me to influence others toward love of you and your holy church.

For Those Advanced in Years

Heavenly Father, your gift is length of days: Help me to make use of mind and body in my advancing years. As you have pardoned my transgressions, sift ingatherings of my memory that evil may grow dim and good may shine forth. I bless you for your gifts, and especially for your presence and the love of friends in heaven and on earth. Grant me new ties of friendship, new opportunities of service, joy in the growth and happiness of children, sympathy with those who bear the world's burdens, clear thought, and quiet faith. Teach me to bear infirmities with cheerful patience. Keep me from narrow pride in outgrown ways, blind eyes that will not see the good of change, impatient judgments of the methods and experiments of others. Let your peace rule my spirit through all the trials of my waning powers. Take from me all fear of death, and all despair or undue love of life, that with a glad heart at rest in you I may await your will.

In Time of Temptation

Lord and Master, Jesus Christ, who was tempted as we are, yet without sin: Give me grace to meet this temptation which now assails me and which I would overcome. Enable me to check all evil thoughts and passions, all enticements to self-indulgence or dishonest gain, and to find, like you, my highest satisfaction in the doing of my heavenly Father's will.

For Loyalty in Discipleship

O Jesus Christ, the Lord of all good life, you have called us to help build the city of God: Enrich and purify my life and deepen me in discipleship. Help me daily to know more of you, and through me, by the power of your Spirit, show you to all others. Make me humble, brave, and loving; make me ready for adventure. I do not ask that you keep me safe, but that you keep me loyal, who for us faced death unafraid, and who lives and reigns for ever and ever.

⚜

Teach me, good Lord, to serve you as you deserve, to give and not to count the cost, to fight and not to heed the wounds, to toil and not to seek for rest, to labor and not to ask for any reward, save that of knowing that I do your will.

For Grace in Speech

Help me, O Lord, to keep guard over my lips. Save me from words that hurt, from gossip and slander and lies. Let me speak only to encourage and cheer and to keep people on their feet, so that all my words may minister grace, to your honor and glory.

For Love Toward God

O God, you have prepared for those who love you such good things as surpass our understanding: Pour into my heart such love toward you, that loving you in all things and above all things, I may obtain your promises, which exceed all that I can desire.

⚜

O God you are the light of the minds that know you, the life of the souls that love you, and the strength of the wills that serve you: Help me so to know you that I may truly love you, so to love you that I may fully serve you, whom to serve is perfect freedom.

In Adversity

Almighty God, you promised that when we are passing through the waters you will be with us, and that they shall not overflow us: Be my help and savior now in this time of trouble. I need your grace and strong hand. Uphold me and do not let me fall into despair or bitterness or the mire of self-pity. Renew in me hope and faith; give me the assurance of your presence and courage to face bravely the trials of the days to come.

In Sickness

O God my Father, hold me in your keeping. You have made my body and meant it to be whole. Be with me when I am bewildered by sickness and pain. Let me trust the power of your healing; and above all and through all let me trust your love that does not fail. Give me back, I pray, health and vigor, that I may set my hands again with gladness to the unhindered tasks of life; but if this may not be, then teach me still to serve as best

I can with bent or broken tools. May any suffering I must undergo teach me sympathy with all who suffer, and may every gift of life renewed send me forth with a thankful heart to greater consecration.

In Bereavement

Almighty God, you have taught us that they who mourn shall be comforted: Grant that in all my grief I may turn to you; and because my need is beyond human help, grant me the peace of your consolation and the joy of your love.

⁂

Heavenly Father, to whom all our sorrows are known, grant to me the comfort of your grace in my loss and loneliness. I thank you for the love that has been mine and that even now is mine, since we are still one in you. Give me day by day strength to bear my burden, and help me to live in the light of the world to come until my life's end.

For Peace of Mind

Lord, you know my cares and my fears. Help me to turn them all over to you, who have promised to give rest to our souls. Grant to me now a restful spirit and a peaceful mind, and in quietness and confidence and faith to find a new strength.

A Prayer Attributed to St. Francis

Lord, make me an instrument of your peace. Where there is hatred, let me sow love; where there is injury, pardon; where there is doubt, faith; where there is despair, hope; where there is darkness, light; where there is sadness, joy. O divine Master, grant that I may not so much seek to be consoled as to console; to be understood as to understand; to be loved as to love. For it is in giving that we receive; it is in pardoning that we are pardoned; and it is in dying that we are born to eternal life.

For Guidance of the Holy Spirit

O God, because without you I am not able to please you, mercifully grant that your Holy Spirit may in all things direct and rule my heart.

For a Time of Decision

Heavenly Father, you have promised the gift of your Holy Spirit to those who ask it: I come to you for light and direction now as I face the necessity of decision between the ways that lie before me. May your Holy Spirit guide me in my uncertainty, saving me from self-will and the placing of desire before responsibility. Let it be your will, not mine, that I seek, and show me how I can both serve you and fulfill my duty toward those dependent upon me. Give me wisdom in this hour, O Lord; and when I see your way, give me grace to follow in it.

For Today

O God:

Give me strength to live another day;
Let me not turn coward before its difficulties or prove recreant to its duties;
Let me not lose faith in other people;
Keep me sweet and sound of heart, in spite of ingratitude, treachery, or meanness;
Preserve me from minding little stings or giving them;
Help me to keep my heart clean, and to live so honestly and fearlessly that no outward failure can dishearten me or take away the joy of conscious integrity;
Open wide the eyes of my soul that I may see good in all things;
Grant me this day some new vision of thy truth;
Inspire me with the spirit of joy and gladness; and make me the cup of strength to suffering souls; in the name of the strong Deliverer, our only Lord and Savior, Jesus Christ.

Prayers for
Guidance
and Surrender

Psalm 25:3-11

Show me your ways, O LORD,
   and teach me your paths.

Lead me in your truth and teach me,
   for you are the God of my salvation;
   in you have I trusted all the day long.

Remember, O LORD, your compassion
       and love,
   for they are from everlasting.

Remember not the sins of my youth
       and my transgressions;
   remember me according to your love
   and for the sake of your goodness,
       O LORD.

Gracious and upright is the LORD;
   therefore he teaches sinners in his way.

He guides the humble in doing right
   and teaches his way to the lowly.
All the paths of the LORD are love and
       faithfulness
   to those who keep his covenant and
       his testimonies.

For your Name's sake, O Lord,
    forgive my sin, for it is great.

Who are they who fear the Lord?
    he will teach them the way that they
                should choose.

Psalm 131

O Lord, I am not proud;
    I have no haughty looks.

I do not occupy myself with great matters,
    or with things that are too hard for me.

But I still my soul and make it quiet,
like a child upon its mother's breast;
    my soul is quieted within me.

O Israel, wait upon the Lord,
    from this time forth for evermore.

Psalm 43:3-6

Send out your light and your truth,
            that they may lead me,
   and bring me to your holy hill
   and to your dwelling;

That I may go to the altar of God,
to the God of my joy and gladness;
   and on the harp I will give thanks
            to you, O God my God.

Why are you so full of heaviness,
            O my soul?
   and why are you so disquieted within me?

Put your trust in God;
   for I will yet give thanks to him,
   who is the help of my countenance,
            and my God.

Eternal Lord of all things, I make my offering, with your favor and help. I make it in the presence of your infinite goodness, and of your glorious Mother, and of all the holy men and women in your heavenly court. I wish and desire, and it is my deliberate decision, provided only that it is for your greater service and praise, to imitate you in bearing all injuries and affronts, and any poverty, actual as well as spiritual, if your most holy Majesty desires to choose and receive me into such a life and state.

—*Ignatius Loyola*

Lord, be thy word my rule;
    in it may I rejoice;
thy glory be my aim,
    thy holy will my choice;
thy promises my hope;
    thy providence my guard;
thine arm my strong support;
    thy self my great reward.

—*Christopher Wordsworth*

O God of peace, who has taught us that in returning and rest we shall be saved, in quietness and in confidence shall be our strength: By the might of your Spirit lift us to your presence, where we may be still and know that you are God.

My Lord and my God, I am thine; keep me thine for ever; uphold my goings in thy paths to the end. Shed abroad thy love in my heart, by the Holy Ghost, more and more; and knowing and believing the love which thou hast towards me, may that love constrain me every day not to live to myself, but to him who died for me. In the hour of temptation succor me; amidst the scorn of evil men sustain my soul, that I may never deny my Lord and Savior, but ever tread in his steps, and wear his image, and glory in him, till the day of his appearing and return, in the glory of his Father. Hear me for his sake.

—*Edward Bickersteth*

O Jesus, I Have Promised

O Jesus, I have promised
    to serve thee to the end;
Be thou forever near me,
    my Master and my friend.
I shall not fear the battle,
    if thou art by my side,
Nor wander from the pathway,
    if thou wilt be my guide.

O let me feel thee near me;
    the world is ever near;
I see the sights that dazzle,
    the tempting sounds I hear.
My foes are ever near me,
    around me and within;
But, Jesus, draw thou nearer,
    and shield my soul from sin.

O let me hear thee speaking
    in accents clear and still,
Above the storms of passion,
    the murmurs of self-will.

O speak to reassure me,
    to hasten or control;
O speak, and make me listen,
    thou guardian of my soul.

O Jesus, thou hast promised
    to all who follow thee,
That where thou art in glory
    there shalt thy servant be;
And, Jesus, I have promised
    to serve thee to the end;
O give me grace to follow,
    my Master and my friend.

O let me see thy foot-marks
    and in them plant mine own;
My hope to follow duly,
    is in thy strength alone;
O guide me, call me, draw me,
    uphold me to the end;
And then in heav'n receive me,
    my Savior and my friend.

                                  —John Ernest Bode

My Lord God, I have no idea where I am going. I do not see the road ahead of me. I cannot know for certain where it will end. Nor do I really know myself, and the fact that I think that I am following your will does not mean that I am actually doing so. But I believe that the desire to please you does in fact please you. And I hope I have that desire in all that I am doing. I hope that I will never do anything apart from that desire. And I know that if I do this you will lead me by the right road though I may know nothing about it. Therefore will I trust you always though I may seem to be lost and in the shadow of death. I will not fear, for you are ever with me, and you will never leave me to face my perils alone.

—*Thomas Merton*

You, Lord, are all I want or need. Use this little creature as you wish. All is yours, all is from you and all is for you. I have no longer anything to look after or to do. Not a single moment is mine to control, for everything is yours. I try neither to add anything to my stature nor to take anything away; nor am I to inquire into or reflect upon anything. It is for you to deal with everything. Holiness, perfection, salvation, spiritual direction, penance—these are all your business. Mine is to be content with you and not adopt any line of action or involve myself in any attachment, but to leave all to your good pleasure.

—*Jean-Pierre de Caussade*

Take, Lord, and receive all my liberty, my memory, my understanding, my will— all that I have and possess. You, Lord, have given all to me. I now give it back to you, O Lord. All of it is yours. Dispose of it according to your will. Give me love of yourself along with your grace, for that is enough for me.

—*Ignatius Loyola*

Take my life, and let it be
    consecrated, Lord, to thee;
Take my moments and my days,
    let them flow in ceaseless praise.
Take my hands, and let them move
    at the impulse of thy love;
Take my feet, and let them be
    swift and beautiful for thee.

Take my voice, and let me sing
    always, only, for my King;
Take my lips, and let them be
    filled with messages from thee.
Take my silver and my gold;
    not a mite would I withhold.
Take my intellect, and use
    every power as thou shalt choose.

Take my will, and make it thine;
    it shall be no longer mine.
Take my heart, it is thine own;
    it shall be thy royal throne.
Take my love; my Lord, I pour
    at thy feet its treasure store.

Take myself, and I will be
    ever, only, all for thee.
                    —*Frances Ridley Havergal*

O most blessed Truth, to you I commit
this decision, for you know all things, and
your will is my peace. Deliver me from the
false choices that come from self-interest,
cowardice, and lack of faith in you, and give
me vision and strength to do your will.
                            —*Margaret Cropper*

Spirit of the Living God

Spirit of the living God,
    fall afresh on me.
Spirit of the living God,
    fall afresh on me.
Break me, melt me,
    mold me, fill me.
Spirit of the living God,
    fall afresh on me.
                        —*Dan Iverson*

Sanctify me within and without: wash me, and I shall be whiter than snow. Let thy truth and thy Spirit meet together in my soul, that my prayer may enter into thy presence; and that thine ear may incline unto my humble petitions: so shall I declare thy loving-kindness in the morning, and thy truth in the night. Good Father, enlighten me and teach my heart rightly to conceive, and my tongue freely to speak, what may be to thy glory and the comfort of thy people: allure me to seek thee, and grant that my heart may rejoice in thee and that I may live and die in thee.

—*John Norden (adapted)*

O Father of light, shine upon my path, that the way before me may be illumined by your brightness. Lift from my heart all anxiety and fear, and teach me to trust you both for what I see and for what is hidden from me. So evermore lead me in your way and keep me in your peace.

Almighty and eternal God, so draw my heart to you, so guide my mind, so fill my imagination, so control my will, that I may be wholly yours, utterly dedicated to you; and then use me as you will, and always to your glory and the welfare of your people.

Lord, lift thou up the light of thy countenance upon me, that in thy light I may see light: The light of thy grace today, and the light of thy glory hereafter.

—*Lancelot Andrewes*

Direct me, O Lord, in all my doings with your most gracious favor, and further me with your continual help; that in all my works begun, continued, and ended in you, I may glorify your holy Name, and finally, by your mercy, obtain everlasting life.

Almighty God, in whom is no darkness at all: Grant me your light perpetually, and when I cannot see the way before me, may I continue to put my trust in you; that so, being guided and guarded by your love, I may be kept from falling, this day and all my days, through Jesus Christ my Lord.

—*William Knight*

Tune thou my harp;
There is not, Lord, could never be,
The skill in me.

Tune thou my harp;
That it may play thy melody,
Thy harmony.

Tune thou my harp;
O Spirit, breathe thy thought through me,
As pleaseth thee.

—*Amy Carmichael*

O God, by whom the meek are guided in judgment, and light rises up in darkness for the godly: Grant me, in all my doubts and uncertainties, the grace to ask what you would have me to do, that the Spirit of wisdom may save me from all false choices, and that in your light I may see light, and in your straight path may not stumble.

I am no longer my own, but thine. Put me to what thou wilt, rank me with whom thou wilt. Put me to doing, put me to suffering. Let me be deployed by thee or laid aside for thee, exalted for thee or brought low for thee. Let me be full, let me be empty. Let me have all things, let me have nothing. I freely and heartily yield all things to thy pleasure and disposal. And now, O glorious and blessed God, Father, Son, and Holy Spirit, thou art mine, and I am thine. So be it. And the covenant which I have made on earth, let it be ratified in heaven. Amen.

—*John Wesley*

Lead, Kindly Light

Lead, kindly Light, amid the
        encircling gloom,
  lead thou me on!
The night is dark, and I am far from home—
    lead thou me on!
Keep thou my feet; I do not ask to see
the distant scene—one step enough for me.

I was not ever thus, nor prayed that thou
    shouldst lead me on.
I loved to choose and see my path; but now
    lead thou me on!
I loved the garish day, and, spite of fears,
pride ruled my will: remember not
        past years.

So long thy power hath blest me, sure it still
    will lead me on,
O'er moor and fen, o'er crag and torrent, till
    the night is gone;
And with the morn those angel faces smile
which I have loved long since,
        and lost awhile.

                  —John Henry Newman

Intercessions

Plan for Intercessions
for a Week

Sunday: For your church: the clergy, lay leaders, teachers and children in church school, choir, women's organizations, secretaries, and sextons.

Monday: For your home, family and relations, and friends.

Tuesday: For the advancement of the kingdom of God, all Christian leaders, and all Christian churches.

Wednesday: For your city and community: the police, firefighters, letter carriers, and all other civic employees.

Thursday: For the country: the President, national and state legislators; the men and women in the armed forces; leaders in industry and labor, and for cooperation and goodwill between them; and all who toil with hand or head.

Friday: For nations and peoples: the United Nations, for the end of rivalry and strife, and the achievement of lasting peace.

Saturday: For the sick and all the poor and suffering throughout the world: the handicapped, the seemingly incurable, the blind and deaf and mute; widows and orphans; doctors, nurses, orderlies, chaplains, and all who work in hospitals; the aged, displaced persons throughout the world, and those in prisons.

For Individuals

For Absent Ones and Travelers

O God, you are present in every place: We pray you to enfold with your loving care our dear ones who are away from us, and all who travel by land, sea, air, or in space. Let your fatherly hand ever be over them; prosper them in their way; grant to them daily strength for their needs; and inspire in them an unwavering faith in you, that they may live always to your honor and glory.

For Those Shut-in and Isolated

We pray you, Lord, for all who are in isolated places or by infirmity are confined to home or hospital. Bless them and grant to them a full and consoling sense of your presence, that together with us they may be strengthened and uplifted by the gift of your grace.

For Orphans and the Homeless

Lord Jesus, who in the days of your flesh had no place to lay your head, look with compassion upon all homeless folk and all children left without parental care. So that we do not fail them in their loneliness and need, inflame the hearts of your people with a spirit of concern for their welfare. Bless all homes for orphans, and all who work for the relief of human distress.

For the Blind and Deaf and Mute

Almighty God, in whose holy Word is a promise of a day when the eyes of the blind shall be opened, the ears of the deaf unstopped, and the tongue of the mute shall sing of thy mercy: Be present to all who now live in darkness or in silence. Fortify them to bear their affliction with unwavering faith; grant to them that inner sight and hearing to which your truth and beauty are ever revealed; and may they know you as their constant friend and guide.

For Alcoholics and Other Addicts

Gracious God, the helper of all who put their trust in you, we pray for those who are enslaved by alcohol or by drugs, especially _____. Give them, O Lord, the will to be free, and the grace to continue in the right way; and show us how to help them and to lead them to you who are our hope and strength.

For the Sick

Heavenly Father, whose blessed Son our Lord took upon himself our infirmities and had compassion upon all sick and suffering: Hear our prayer for all who suffer in body or mind or spirit; and especially we pray for _____. Grant to them relief from pain, strength in their weakness, light in their darkness and, if it shall please you, restoration to health. Enable them now to trust you though your way is hidden from their sight; and let them know that peace which is the gift of your Holy Spirit.

For a Sick Child

Heavenly Father, who sent your beloved Son into the world in the form of a little child, and to whom all children are dear: Watch with us over _____. In your mercy ease *his* suffering and restore *him* to health again. Bless those who minister to *his* needs, and give to us who wait the help of your grace.

For Those Who Serve the Sick

Blessed Lord, you went about doing good and healing all manner of sickness and infirmity. Bestow your blessing, we pray, upon our doctors and nurses and all who work in hospitals and homes for the relief of human suffering. Give them skill and tenderness, cheerfulness and patience, and let them find their reward in grateful hearts and in the knowledge that they are serving you.

For the Seemingly Incurable

O Lord, you feel the pain of the world: Look with mercy, we pray, upon those who in their sickness and suffering are beyond the reach of human skill. To you alone belongs the power of life, and these souls are yours. If in the mystery of your providence it shall be their lot to bear their infirmity to the end, then, Lord, of your love give them grace to endure bravely, and such an assurance of your presence with them in it that they may, like their Savior, be made perfect through suffering.

For the Dying

Father of mercies and God of all comfort, we commit to your gracious care and keeping this dear soul whose earthly day is ending and who is going from us to you. Receive *him*, Lord, whose hope is in you. Forgive *his* sins and confirm in *him* the fullness of joy and peace in continuing service in your heavenly kingdom.

For the Departed

O God, whose mercies cannot be numbered, accept our prayers on behalf of the soul of your servant departed, and grant *him* an entrance into the land of light and joy, in the fellowship of your saints.

Remember your servant, O Lord, according to the favor which you bear unto your people, and grant that, increasing in knowledge and love of you, *he* may go from strength to strength, in the life of perfect service in your heavenly kingdom.

Rest eternal grant to *him*, O Lord; and let light perpetual shine upon *him*.

For Those Who Mourn

Grant, O Lord, to all who are bereaved the spirit of faith and courage, that they may have strength to meet the days to come with steadfastness and patience; not sorrowing as those without hope, but in thankful remembrance of your great goodness in past years, and in the sure expectation of a joyful reunion with those they love.

For Animals

O God, you have made all the earth and every creature that dwells in it: Help us, we pray, to treat with compassion the living creatures entrusted to our care, that they may not suffer from our neglect nor become the victims of any cruelty. Bless all who serve in their behalf, and help us to find in caring for them a deeper understanding of your love for all creation.

For the Church

For the Church

O Eternal God, who by your Son Jesus Christ established the family of your church in all the world: Breathe upon it anew the gifts of your Holy Spirit, that, ever awake to your command, it may go forth in lowly service, yet in conquering might, to win the world to the love of your Name.

Quicken, O Lord, we pray you, all members of your church, that they may be alive to the opportunities and responsibilities of our times. Save us from complacency and from fear of new ways; inspire our minds with the vision of a world won for you; and stir our wills to pray and to work until your will is done on earth as it is in heaven.

For a Local Church

O God, you have brought us into the fellowship of your dear Son: Lead us all in this church ever closer day by day to you and to one another, that we may become of one heart and mind in love toward you; and grant that our common life and work in sacrificial service may help to extend your kingdom here and in all the world.

For Church Councils

Almighty God, by whose Holy Spirit the apostles were guided in their councils: Direct, we pray, the deliberations of our leaders and those who share with them the responsibility of planning and providing for the ongoing work of our church. Grant to them wise judgment and adventurous faith, that they may lead us ever forward to greater service and achievement in the furtherance of your kingdom in the world, until your will is done on earth as it is in heaven and all peoples are one united family in you.

For Church Organizations

O Lord, whose holy apostle has taught us that as members of your body we all have our part to play in the life of your church: We thank you for this work which you have given us to do together. Grant us grace to persevere in it, and through it to serve you to your honor and glory.

For the Clergy

O Lord Jesus Christ, the Good Shepherd, you laid down your life for the sheep and appointed others to feed your flock: Give our pastors and other clergy the grace they need day by day faithfully to carry out the demanding duties of their sacred calling. Fill them with love for the souls committed to their care; inspire them with wisdom for the guidance and instruction of those who seek their aid; and in all things help them and us whom they serve to glorify you by the good example of Christian lives.

For Church Officers

Blessed Lord, you have called us to this office in your church: Guide us in our deliberations, so that all our aims and purposes may be to the strengthening of the work in this church and the support of the church's mission throughout the world.

For Lay Workers

O Lord Jesus Christ, to whose service we are dedicated in your holy church, fit us for the work we are given to do. Enlighten our minds as we study your holy Word; inspire us as we teach and preach; and make us good examples to others in holiness of life, to your honor and glory.

Dedication of Church School Teachers and Officers

Father of mercy, whose blessed Son, our Lord, laid upon his disciples the care and well-being of children: We pray for your blessing upon these persons who have offered themselves for the service of Christian nurture in our church school. We thank you for the privilege that is theirs and ours in sharing in this early training of our children in Christian faith and life. Endue them with insight and understanding, with patience and love; and when the going is hard, grant to them the secret joy that comes of faithful continuance in the task undertaken.

For Church Schools

O God, our heavenly Father, through your Son our Lord Jesus Christ you have made known your tender care for children: Grant your blessing, we pray, upon our church schools. To those who teach give intelligence and patience, and to those who are taught the desire to learn and the will to walk in the way of your commandments.

For Theological Schools

Almighty God, our heavenly Father, the only Source of light and life: Send down upon our theological schools the rich gifts of your good Spirit, that in them your truth may be sincerely sought, effectually received, and obediently followed, and that in growing measure they may become centers of inspiration and power. Strengthen their teachers with wisdom, zeal, and patience; inspire their scholars with the spirit of truth, honor, and humility; and grant that all members of the church they serve may give them willing and generous support.

For Those in Religious Communities

Blessed Lord, you called your disciples to follow you in the way of sacrifice: We remember before you those who have forsaken the natural pleasures and ambitions of life to devote themselves entirely to prayer and the service of your holy church. In their poverty, chastity, and obedience be their wealth, their strength and stay, that in all things they may please you and show forth your glory before all the world.

For Missionaries

O most merciful Savior, you desire that all should be saved: Be present with those who are gone forth in your Name to preach the gospel in distant lands (especially _____). Be with them in all perils, in sickness and distress, in weariness and pain, in disappointment and persecution. Give them sure confidence in you. Pour out abundantly upon them your Holy Spirit, and prosper mightily the work of their hands. Send to them faithful and true fellow-laborers. Give them a rich increase here, and grant that hereafter they may dwell with you in the heavenly places, world without end.

For Mission Hospitals

O Lord, the healer of all our diseases, you know how the sick have need of a physician: Let your perpetual providence guide and direct the work of mission hospitals throughout the world. Strengthen all whom you have called to be sharers in your own work of healing, that the pain and grief of the world may be lightened and the bounds of your kingdom enlarged.

For Educational Missions

O God, the goal of all knowledge and the source of all truth, you lead humanity toward yourself along the paths of discovery and learning: Direct with your wise Spirit the work of education in every land. Especially we pray for those with the difficult task of proclaiming the gospel in terms understandable to peoples of different cultures. Give them insight into the needs of those whom they teach, humility to learn from their traditions, and wisdom to combine the old and the new. Above all, give them that grace and beauty of life without which all knowledge is vain.

For Church Unity

O God, our heavenly Father, whose blessed Son came to bring us all into one family in you: We pray for the unity of the church in the world. Help us to seek to heal the divisions which keep us from one another and weaken our efforts to extend your kingdom on earth. Give us understanding of other peoples' points of view, save us from prejudice, and grant that as we see clearly our Savior's will that his church may be one, so we may labor in love to bring it to pass.

O God, you have established the foundations of your church upon the holy mountains: Grant that the church may not be moved by any wiles of error which seek its overthrow, nor be shaken by earthly disputes and disquietude, but ever stand fast upon the teachings of the apostles, in the spirit of service and humility.

—*adapted from Leo the Great*

Lord Jesus Christ, who prayed that all your children might be one: We pray for the restoration of unity in your church. Forgive the pride and suspicion which have driven us apart. Take away our narrow-mindedness, our bitterness, our prejudice, our inability to see you in the face of our brother. May we never consider as normal the disunity which is a scandal to the world and an affront to your love. Teach us to recognize the gifts of your grace in all who call upon you through Jesus Christ our Lord.

—*from the French Reformed Church Liturgy*

For the Nation

Almighty God, look with favor upon our land and people. All undeserving, you have made us great among the nations of the earth. Let us not forget that this place and this power have come from you, and that we have them as a trust to use in your service. Save us from pride and arrogance; make us quick to see the needs of those less fortunate than ourselves, and to be resolute in promoting goodwill and fellowship among all people.

For the World

Almighty God, give us the will to labor for harmony and cooperation among the nations of the world. Put away from us all prejudice and all selfish ambition; and in our foreign policy help us to pursue only those ends and purposes that will promote unity and concord and further the coming of your kingdom in the earth.

For the United Nations

Eternal God, we pray for all who serve in the United Nations. Grant your blessing upon their endeavors to heal the wounds of the world through cooperation in education and other fields of human service. May your Holy Spirit so guide their deliberations in Council and Assembly, that all causes of strife may be removed, and peace and concord be secured among all the peoples of the earth.

For a Just Social Order

O God, holy and just, you exalt a nation that follows the way of righteousness: We pray for our land and people that we may become worthy of your gracious favor. Deliver us from greed of gain, from race and class prejudice and ill-will, from all causes of discontent and strife. Inspire in us such love of our neighbor and concern for one another's welfare that we shall work together with one heart and will to secure equality of opportunity and due reward for all.

For Immigrants and Exiles

Dear Lord, our Father, you have made of one blood all the nations upon the earth and called all people your children: Bless all immigrants and exiles, and especially those who have come to this land. May their coming be a blessing to the nation and to them. Help us to labor together with them in fellowship to build here a righteous society founded on brotherhood and justice. We ask all in the Name of him through whom your kingdom comes.

For the Poor and the Neglected

Almighty and most merciful God, we remember before you all poor and neglected persons whom it would be easy for us to forget: the homeless and the destitute, the old and the sick, and all who have none to care for them. Help us to heal those who are broken in body or spirit, and to turn their sorrow into joy. Grant this, Father, for the love of your Son, who for our sake became poor, Jesus Christ our Lord.

For Those Who
Serve the Nation

For Those in Authority

Lord God Almighty, guide our President and all those to whom has been committed the government of this nation. Grant to them gifts of wisdom and understanding, of counsel and strength, that upholding what is right and following what is true, they may obey your holy will and fulfill your divine purpose.

For Officers of the State

We commend to you, O Lord, all who are engaged in the government of this state. Grant to them integrity of purpose and unfailing devotion to the cause of justice. May all their legislation promote our welfare, to the succor of the poor, the relief of the oppressed, the putting down of social evils, and the redress of social wrongs, to your glory and the good example of your people.

For Our Armed Forces

Heavenly Father, we commend to your gracious care and keeping all the men and women in our armed forces at home and abroad. Defend them day by day with your heavenly grace; strengthen them in their trials and temptations; give them courage to face the perils that beset them; and help them to know that none can pluck out of your hand those who put their trust in you.

For Social Agencies

Almighty God, your compassion does not fail and you have taught us to have compassion upon those in need: Prosper, we pray you, the work of all social relief agencies. Stir up the wills of all people to support them in the relief of want and suffering, and let us not rest until we have provided for the needs of your children, giving generously as you have given to us.

O Lord, we pray that you will hasten the time when no one shall live in contentment while a neighbor has need. Inspire in us and in all people the consciousness that we are not our own but yours and our neighbors', for his sake who prayed that we might all be one in him, Christ Jesus our Lord.

For Goodwill in Industry

Father of all, you sent your only Son to bring peace on earth, goodwill toward all: Fulfill the purpose of his coming by increasing goodwill and preserving peace between employers and employed. To all who lead in industry and labor give the desire to seek not power and privilege for themselves but the common good of all, that by justice, mutual consideration, and faithful work, they may advance our national well-being.

For Workers

O God, Father of us all, we pray for those who toil in mill or mine, for those by whose labor we are clothed and fed, for those who work in the darkness of the earth, for those who build and adorn our houses, for those who trade in shop or market, and for those who travel by land, sea, and air. May our service and our merchandise be holy unto the Lord. May we do justly and love mercy and walk humbly with you.

For Teachers

O God, our heavenly Father, we pray for those whose lives are spent in teaching or in other service in our schools and colleges. Grant them strength to carry them through their tasks, and let them see the reward of their labors in sound Christian character and good citizenship.

For Schools, Colleges, and Universities

Almighty God, behold our universities, colleges, and schools with your gracious favor, that knowledge may be increased among us and all good learning flourish and abound. Bless all who teach and all who learn; and grant that in humility of heart they may ever look to you, the fountain of all wisdom.

For a Medical School

Almighty God, you have made us in your own image and called us to be workers together with you in your eternal purpose: We pray for your blessing upon all who serve you and humanity in the healing arts and sciences, and especially those who teach and those who learn and labor in this school. You who created medicines for our use and succor, hear our prayer for those whose lives are dedicated to the relief of pain and suffering and to the gift of health. Grant to them insight and ingenuity in discovery, integrity and skill in the use of their knowledge and their powers, and strength of mind and body for the constant demands of their high calling.

For Strength to Persevere

O Lord Jesus Christ, who when on earth was ever about thy Father's business: Grant that we may not grow weary in well-doing. Give us grace to do all in thy name. Be thou the beginning and the end of all: the pattern whom we follow, the redeemer in whom we trust, the master whom we serve, the friend to whom we look for sympathy. May we never shrink from our duty from any fear of man. Make us faithful unto death; and bring us at last into the eternal presence, where with the Father and the Holy Ghost thou livest and reignest for ever.

—*E. B. Pusey*

Special
Occasions

Before a Journey or
New Undertaking

Lord, we pray that you will be with us and keep us as we go upon this journey (*or* enter upon this new undertaking). Let no change or chance take us out of your hand; prosper us in our way, and give us grace always to do the things that will please you.

For the New Year

O God, our Heavenly Father, as we enter upon this new year we commit ourselves to your faithful care and keeping. Give us the grace so to love you with all our heart and mind and strength that we may live without fear, and so to love our neighbors as ourselves that we may live without reproach. Grant that no chance or change may turn us aside from the doing of your holy will.

Before a Marriage

O God, our heavenly Father, we pray for your grace and blessing as we take upon ourselves the sacred vows of Christian marriage. Let our love for each other be pure and enduring; give us understanding of each other's mind and needs; help us to share our joys and sorrows; and keep us ever faithful to our promise to live together according to your will till death shall separate us.

For a Mother
Awaiting Childbirth

Lord Jesus Christ, whose blessed Mother knew the joy of anticipation as well as the fears of childbirth: Grant me the grace of a quiet mind during these days of waiting, and the strength and courage that I shall need when the time of delivery is near. And may the child that shall be born to me bring blessing, and be a blessing always.

Thanksgiving After Childbirth

Heavenly Father, we thank you that you have been with us and kept us through the pain and peril of childbirth, and that we can now rejoice in this child which has been born into the world. We bless you for all your mercies, and pray that in the days to come we may prove worthy of this great gift which you have bestowed upon us.

On the Adoption of a Child

Our Father, you have bestowed upon us this great privilege of taking to ourselves as one of our own one of your little ones to love and care for, and to bring up in your faith and fear: Grant us, we pray, the grace to give to *him* the full measure of our devotion, and to set before *him* always a good example of Christian life. Bless us in our growth together, and may our home be enriched in the simple joys that come of loving and serving one another.

Before the Baptism of a Child

O God, our Father, we thank you for our child; and as we take *him* to *his* baptism in your holy church we pray you to receive *him* into the arms of your love and to keep *him* ever in your watchful care. Give us grace to help *him* grow in grace, both by our own good example and by instruction in the teachings of the church, and may *he* remain a faithful soldier and servant of our Lord Jesus Christ, to his life's end.

For Godparents and Sponsors

Heavenly Father, you have called me to this high privilege and responsibility as a *godfather (godmother)* for _____. Help me to be worthy of it, and to do my duty faithfully through the years to come. Bless _____ and grant that *he* may become a faithful follower of Christ and a loyal member of the church, and that we may both continue yours for ever, until we come at last to your everlasting kingdom.

Before Confirmation

O God, whose child I was made in Holy Baptism, be with me and bless me in my Confirmation. As I renew the vows that were made for me, and make my promise to follow Jesus Christ as my Lord and Savior, may your Holy Spirit give me strength to keep it, and the will to be a loyal member of the church all the days of my life.

For a Wedding Anniversary

Heavenly Father, we give you heartfelt thanks on this anniversary of the day when we were made one in Holy Matrimony; for your blessing upon us then, and for your continual mercies until now. We thank you that our love has deepened with the passing of days, and for all the joys of our home and family life. Renew your blessing upon us now, as we renew our vows of love and loyalty, and may your Holy Spirit strengthen us that we may ever remain steadfast in our faith and in your service.

Before an Operation

Dear God, I commend myself, body and soul, to your gracious care and keeping. Give to me a restful spirit and a quiet mind, and the patience to await without complaint the return of health.

Thanksgiving After Recovery

Almighty God, in whose hands are all our ways: I thank you that in your mercy I have come safely through my sickness and have my health again. Help me now to show my thankfulness to you by serving you more faithfully in my daily life and by sharing more sacrificially in the work of your holy church.

On the Death of a Child

O Lord Jesus Christ, who took little children into your arms and blessed them, open our eyes to see our child now in the arms of your infinite love. Comfort us who mourn, and grant that we may so love and serve you in this life, that together with *him* we may obtain the fullness of your promises in the world to come.

On the Death of a Young Man or Woman

O Lord Jesus Christ, you knew on earth the joy and vigor of youth: Grant to *him* whom we love a welcome into your service, that *he* may share with you in the abundant life of your eternal kingdom.

At the Burial of One in the Profession of the Arts

We thank you, Lord, for all who have served their generation in the pursuits of the arts: for all who in word and sound and form and color have increased the joy of life, and especially for your servant and our friend _____. We pray that *he* may find fulfillment in your eternal kingdom, where the beautiful, the good, and the true alone are found for evermore.

For the Anniversary of
One Departed

Almighty God, we remember before you this day *him* to whom we are bound in the bond of love, and we pray that *he* may ever find fulfillment in the joyful service of your heavenly kingdom.

For a Business or Service Club

Almighty God, whose great commandment is that we shall love our neighbors as ourselves, and who has taught us that we should do to others as we would have them do to us: We ask your blessing upon the work of this club. As our purpose is to help others and to promote all that is good in our community, so we pray that you will strengthen our hands in all our undertakings, and that our work may spread the spirit of fellowship and goodwill everywhere.

For a Commencement

Prosper, O Lord, the work of all our schools and colleges. Grant that all who teach and learn may set your holy will ever before them, and seek that wisdom and understanding which are better than the riches of the world. And especially we pray for the blessing upon this school and upon those who now pass from its walls into new spheres of learning and work. May your fatherly hand ever be over them and your Holy Spirit ever be with them. Lead them in the way of truth and of honorable service, until they come to your everlasting kingdom.

For a Clergy Conference

O Lord Jesus Christ, Head of your body the church, by whom we have been chosen as ambassadors and ministers of reconciliation: Direct us in all our doings with your most gracious favor; let all our plans and purposes be in accordance with your holy will, our aim only that we may serve you and your people faithfully as good shepherds of your flock.

Enlighten us by your Holy Spirit as we consider together the meaning and obligations of our sacred calling and the opportunities and responsibilities of the church in these times. Inspire our minds, direct our wills, and strengthen our hands, that we may not falter or fail in the work you have given us to do, to your honor and glory.

For a Lay Conference

O God, by your Holy Spirit you endowed men and women with spiritual gifts for service in your church: We thank you that you have called us to help in the extension of your kingdom on the earth. As we seek together now to discover how and where we best can serve you, make known to us your will and give us the spirit of understanding and obedience that as we see what you would have us do, we may devote ourselves wholeheartedly to the doing of it. Keep us faithful to you in our daily lives, and help us in our everyday work to find opportunities to serve you, to your honor and glory.

For a Youth Group
or Conference

O God, our heavenly Father, we pray for your blessing upon all who are joined together in this fellowship of youth. Help us so to think and pray, play and work together, that we may become one in purpose to seek your will for our lives and to serve and enjoy you faithfully.

For a Retreat

O Lord Jesus Christ, who said to your apostles, "Come apart into a desert place and rest awhile," for there were many coming and going: Grant to your servants here gathered that they may rest awhile at this present time with you. May they so seek you, whom their souls desire to love, that they may both find you and be found by you. And grant such love and such wisdom to accompany the words which shall be spoken in your name, that they may not fall to the ground, but may lead us through the toils of our pilgrimage to that rest which remains to the people of God where, nevertheless, they rest not day and night from your perfect service.

For a Mission

Almighty God, who sent your Son into the world to save sinners and to lead us into the way of righteousness: Bestow your blessing upon our endeavor to bring souls to you through this mission, and draw us to deeper consecration. May your Holy Spirit inspire those who shall speak your word, convince the indifferent, convert the wayward, and in all of us renew the will to do your will and to continue steadfastly in your service in the fellowship of your holy church, until your will is done on earth as it is in heaven.

A Birthday Offering for Children

Lord Jesus, you showed your love for children by taking them into your arms and giving them your blessing: Bless also these children now here before you with their gifts of thanksgiving for their birthday. We commend them to your sustaining grace, and pray you will ever be their friend and companion through the years to come, and that they may follow you faithfully to their life's end.

For an Annual Church Meeting

Grant, O Lord, that your Holy Spirit may preside over us now in all our concerns and deliberations for the welfare of this congregation. We thank you for all the blessings of the past year, and pray that we may go together from strength to strength in the year before us. Help us all to dedicate ourselves to you, and to be ready to make sacrifices of time and money for the extension of your kingdom.

Guide us, we pray, in the choice of our officers, and may they discharge their duties faithfully.

We praise you for your servants who labored and worshiped here before us, and especially for those who have departed this life since we last met together. Grant to them eternal rest, O Lord, and let light perpetual shine upon them.

For the Annual Canvass

O God, you have called us to be workers together with you: Make us now of one heart and mind to pray and work and give for the upbuilding and strengthening of your church at home and abroad. Bless our annual canvass, and stir up the wills of all our people to do according to their ability as good stewards in your service.

For a Church Building Campaign

Almighty God, you promised that wherever your Name is recorded you will come with your blessing: Look with favor on our endeavors to build in this place a church worthy of your holy Name. Move the hearts and wills of all to give and serve until our purpose is accomplished, to your honor and glory.

Choosing a New Priest

Almighty God, we pray for the guidance of your Holy Spirit as we seek a new priest for our church. You know our special needs and the task that lies to our hand. Direct us in our search and give us insight to perceive the leader you would choose for us. And we further pray, O Lord, that in this time of waiting we may all devote ourselves afresh to your service, so that nothing be lost of the faithful work of the past, but rather that it may be brought to a rich harvest in the years to come. This we ask in the Name of Jesus Christ our Lord.

Institution of Officers
in a Church Organization

O God, who by your Holy Spirit endowed the early disciples with varying gifts for the upbuilding and extension of the Church, all having a part to play according to their ability: We commend to you now these your servants who have been chosen for the responsible office of _____ in the _____ of this church. Accept, O Lord, the willing offering of their time and talents; may your Holy Spirit enable them to discharge their duties faithfully and well, and make their service fruitful to your honor and glory.

For Dedication of
Church Furnishings

Lord God of our fathers, who of old accepted the willing offerings of your people for the service and the beautifying of the church: We pray you to accept and bless this (these) _____ which we now dedicate for our use and to your glory in our worship of you. We thank you for the faith and devotion of your servant(s) by whom (*or* for whom) these gifts were made; and we commend them to your constant care and keeping.

For a Thanksgiving Day

Almighty God, we thank you for all the blessings of this life, and today especially for those that are ours in this free land: for the fruits of the soil, the untold resources of the earth, the opportunities for work and play and healthful living; for liberty in speech and the written word; for public education and regard for every person's welfare. And we pray that, as we thank you for these and all your mercies, you will continue your good hand upon us and make our nation great in that greatness which alone is pleasing to you, even the righteousness that is the doing of your holy will.

Grace for a Patriotic Banquet

We thank you, Lord, for these your earthly gifts, and for all the blessings of this life. Especially now, we give you thanks for our country, for those who laid its foundations, and for those who have sacrificed their lives in its service. Strengthen, we pray you, those who now labor to keep it strong; and be our defense against all our enemies, so that peace and harmony may ever flourish among us, and spread from us throughout the world.

For a National Observance

We thank you, O Lord, for your continued blessings to our people. We thank you for the pioneers who opened the way, and for those who laid the foundations of our national life. Grant that we may ever dedicate ourselves to the unfinished work they so nobly advanced, and give increased devotion to the cause for which they gave the last full measure of devotion: that government of the people, by the people, for the people, shall not perish from the earth. With malice toward none, with charity for all, with firmness in the right as you give us to see the right, let us strive to finish the work we are in: to bind up the nation's wounds, to care for all who need our care, and to achieve and cherish a just and lasting peace among ourselves and with all nations.

Before an Election

Almighty God, you hold us to account for the use of all our powers and privileges: Guide us, the people of this nation, in the election of our leaders and representatives, that by wise legislation and faithful administration the rights of all may be protected, and our nation enabled to fulfill your purposes.

In a Time of Strife

Lord, give us the grace to put ourselves in other people's places, to see ourselves as others see us. Save us from strife that comes from self-will or lack of understanding, and help us to seek a way to work together for the rights and liberties of all in responsible community life and service. As you are the Father of us all, so let us live as members of one family in mutual consideration and concern for love of you.

In Time
of War

For a Will to Peace

Almighty God, by whose grace we look for the day when nation shall no more lift up sword against nation, and when all people shall live without fear in security and peace: Grant to us in this time of strife the will to labor for peace even while our sword is drawn to resist the oppressor. Let not the evil we oppose turn us from our purpose to achieve unity and concord among the nations of the earth, to your honor and glory.

For Chaplains in the Armed Forces

Blessed Lord, who commissioned your disciples to continue the work which the Father sent you into the world to do: Support with your Holy Spirit those who minister in the armed forces of our country. Give them the grace to preach your gospel both by word and deed; strengthen them in their temptations and make them courageous in the perils of their calling, that they may glorify you before all people; and then, Lord, hold them ever in your gracious keeping.

For the Medical Services

O Lord, merciful Physician of souls, let your blessing rest upon our medical services in the theater of war. Give to the doctors, nurses, stretcher-bearers, orderlies, and Red Cross workers a full measure of your enabling grace, that they may not grow weary in well-doing, but continue steadfastly in their work of mercy; and grant that through their labors many may be saved.

For the Wounded and the Fallen

Heavenly Father, we commit to your gracious keeping the sick and wounded, the missing, and prisoners of war. Be their strength and consolation, and in your love and mercy receive the fallen to yourself, forgiving them their sins for your Name's sake.

For the Bereaved

Almighty God, who offered your only Son to be made perfect through suffering, and to win our salvation by enduring the cross: Sustain with your healing power all whose loved ones have given their lives in the service of our country. Redeem, we pray you, the pain of their bereavement, that knowing their loss to be the price of our freedom, they may remember the gratitude of the nation for which they gave so costly a sacrifice. And grant, O Lord, that these dead shall not have died in vain, and that out of the distress of this present age there may arise a new and better world in which your will shall rule, to the honor of your Son, our Savior Jesus Christ.

For Our Enemies

Lord, remember not only men and women of good will, but also those of ill will. But do not remember the suffering they have inflicted on us; remember the fruits we have bought, thanks to this suffering—our comradeship, our loyalty, our humility, our courage, our generosity, the greatness of heart which has grown out of all this—and when they come to judgment, let the fruits which we have borne be their forgiveness.

—written by an unknown prisoner
in the Ravensbrück Concentration Camp
and left by the body of a dead child.

For Holy
Communion

Prayers of Preparation

LORD, who may dwell in your tabernacle?
who may abide upon your holy hill?

Whoever leads a blameless life and does
what is right,
who speaks the truth from his heart.

There is no guile upon his tongue;
he does no evil to his friend;
he does not heap contempt upon his
neighbor.

In his sight the wicked is rejected,
but he honors those who fear the LORD.

He has sworn to do no wrong
and does not take back his word.

He does not give his money in hope of gain,
nor does he take a bribe against the
innocent.

Whoever does these things
shall never be overthrown.

—Psalm 15

I will go to the altar of God, to the God of my joy and gladness. I will offer the sacrifice of thanksgiving.

The Lord Jesus on the night when he was betrayed took a loaf of bread, and when he had given thanks, he broke it and said, "This is my body that is for you. Do this in remembrance of me." In the same way he took the cup also, after supper, saying, "This cup is the new covenant in my blood. Do this, as often as you drink it, in remembrance of me." For as often as you eat this bread and drink the cup, you proclaim the Lord's death until he comes. Whoever, therefore, eats the bread or drinks the cup of the Lord in an unworthy manner will be answerable for the body and blood of the Lord. Examine yourselves, and only then eat of the bread, and drink of the cup. For all who eat and drink without discerning the body, eat and drink judgment against themselves.

—*1 Corinthians 11:23-29*

Almighty and everlasting God, behold us as we approach the sacrament of your only begotten Son, our Lord Jesus Christ. As sick, we come to the physician of life; as unclean, to the fountain of mercy; as blind, to the light of eternal splendor; as needy, to the Lord of heaven and earth.

We pray you of your infinite mercy to heal our sickness, to wash our foulness, to lighten our darkness, and to enrich our poverty, that we may receive the bread of angels, the King of kings, the Lord of lords, with such reverence and fear, such contrition and love, such faith and purity, such devotion and humility as is expedient for the welfare of our souls. And grant us, most merciful God, so to receive the Body and Blood of your dear Son, Jesus Christ, that we may be incorporated into his mystical body and ever reckoned among his members. And, most loving Father, grant that we may at length behold with open face him whom we now purpose to receive under a veil, your beloved Son, who with you and the Holy Spirit lives and reigns ever, one God, world without end.

꙳

Before the cross of Christ we can only bow in penitence for our great sin, in adoration of the glory which we there behold, full of grace and truth. We pray that as we are judged by the cross, so we may also be pardoned, and that the love of God may so flood our hearts and fill our world that all may be drawn to Christ, their shattered fellowships remade, and deeper and more lasting community established.

꙳

O Savior of the world, who by your cross and precious blood has redeemed us: Save us, and help us, we humbly pray you, O Lord.

On Entering Church

Heavenly Father, bless me and all who worship here and elsewhere today in the fellowship of your holy church. Help me to worship you in spirit and in sincerity, and to receive your holy Word in singleness of heart and mind.

Merciful Father, I humbly approach your altar, desiring to offer you the sacrifice of praise and thanksgiving:
    For your honor and glory,
    In remembrance of the death and
          passion of your Son,
    In intercession for your church,
    With thanksgiving for the grace and
          virtue of all your saints,
    For the pardon of my sins and power
          to lead a new life,
    And for (*here name any special request*
          or intention).
Accept me, O God, and bless me for your Name's sake.

At the Offertory

Come to me, O Lord, in this holy sacrament; feed me with the bread of life, and give me grace to unite myself with you in your self-offering for the salvation of humanity.

Come, Risen Lord

Come, risen Lord, and deign to be our guest;
nay, let us be thy guests; the feast is thine;
thyself at thine own board make manifest
in thine own Sacrament of Bread and Wine.

We meet, as in that upper room they met;
thou at the table, blessing, yet dost stand:
"This is my Body"; so thou givest yet:
faith still receives the cup as from thy hand.

One body we, one Body who partake,
one Church united in communion blest;
one Name we bear, one Bread of life we break,
with all thy saints on earth and saints at rest.

One with each other, Lord, for one in thee,
who art one Savior and one living Head;
then open thou our eyes, that we may see;
be known to us in breaking of the Bread.

—*George Wallace Briggs*

Thou Who at
Thy First Eucharist

Thou, who at thy first Eucharist didst
pray that
all thy Church might be for ever one,
grant us at every Eucharist to say
with longing heart and soul, "Thy will
be done."
O may we all one bread, one body be,
through this blest sacrament of unity.

For all thy Church, O Lord, we intercede;
make thou our sad divisions soon to cease;
draw us the nearer each to each, we plead,
by drawing all to thee, O Prince of Peace;
thus may we all one bread, one body be,
through this blest sacrament of unity.

So, Lord, at length when sacraments
shall cease,
may we be one with all thy Church above,
one with thy saints in one unbroken peace,
one with thy saints in one unbounded love;
more blessed still, in peace and love to be
one with the Trinity in Unity.

—William Harry Turton

Before Going to the Altar

Lord Jesus, eternal Word of God incarnate, who has ascended into heaven yet in the fullness of your presence are with us now, humbly I adore you.

After Holy Communion

Heavenly Father, I pray that this Holy Communion may be to me new life and salvation, an armor of faith and a shield of good resolution, the riddance of evil and the increase of virtue. Be my hope and confidence, my riches and my joy, my refuge and my help, in whom my heart and mind may remain forever fixed.

On Leaving Church

Grant, O Lord, that the lessons I have learned may take root in my heart, that I may remain faithful to the confession of the faith and, aided by your continuing grace, may put my faith to practice in my daily life.

Litanies and
Meditations

Litanies

Litany of the Christian Life

These are the words of the holy apostles:

Let the same mind be in you that was in Christ Jesus who...emptied himself, taking the form of a slave...humbled himself, and became obedient to the point of death—even death on a cross.

—*Philippians 2:5-8*

Lord, have mercy upon us, and give us the mind of Christ.

Bear one another's burdens, and in this way you will fulfill the law of Christ.

—*Galatians 6:2*

Lord, have mercy upon us, and give us the mind of Christ.

How does God's love abide in anyone who has the world's goods and sees a brother or sister in need and yet refuses help? Little children, let us love, not in word or speech, but in truth and action.

—*1 John 3:17-18*

Lord, have mercy upon us, and give us the mind of Christ.

Religion that is pure and undefiled before God, the Father, is this: to care for orphans and widows in their distress, and to keep oneself unstained by the world.

—*James 1:27*

Lord, have mercy upon us, and give us the mind of Christ.

Support your faith with goodness, and goodness with knowledge, and knowledge with self-control, and self-control with endurance, and endurance with godliness, and godliness with mutual affection, and mutual affection with love.

—*2 Peter 1:5-7*

Lord, have mercy upon us, and give us the mind of Christ.

Beloved, build yourselves up on your most holy faith; pray in the Holy Spirit; keep yourselves in the love of God; look forward to the mercy of our Lord Jesus Christ that leads to eternal life.

—Jude 20

Lord, have mercy upon us, and give us the mind of Christ.

A Litany of Remembrance

Heavenly Father, we wait upon you now in trust and love, and in filial devotion to your holy will. By all your works, by the remembrance of all your mercies, by the revelation of yourself to the prophets of old:

Teach us, and draw us ever nearer to you.

By the memory of Jesus Christ our Lord, by his life and teaching, by his life laid down for our salvation, by the work of his Spirit in the world:

Teach us, and draw us ever nearer to you.

By the noble example of all the saints and martyrs of the church, by all that we owe to Christian faith and devotion down the years:

Teach us, and draw us ever nearer to you.

By the joys of life, by human love, by the affection and fidelity of friends, by the capacity for pleasure and the sense of humor, by the persistence of hope in our hearts:

Teach us, and draw us ever nearer to you.

By the sorrows of life, by our falls and failures, by our disappointments and disasters, by the stern discipline of loneliness, of unrealized dreams, and the heartache of unsatisfied desire:

Teach us, and draw us ever nearer to you.

By our want of you, by the hunger within us for the eternal life, by our search for truth, and by our hands outstretched in prayer:

Teach us, and draw us ever nearer to you.

Say The Lord's Prayer

Litany of the Will of God

Jesus said: Not everyone who says to me, "Lord, Lord," will enter the kingdom of heaven, but only the one who does the will of my Father in heaven.

—*Matthew 7:21*

For whoever does the will of my Father in heaven is my brother and sister and mother.

—*Matthew 12:50*

O God, you have made us for yourself and called us to work with you in your eternal purpose:

Your will be done on earth as it is in heaven.

O God, you will that your Name and salvation be known in all the world:

Your will be done on earth as it is in heaven.

O God, you desire that all should know the truth that sets them free:

Your will be done on earth as it is in heaven.

O God, your purpose is to draw all people together as one family in Christ:

Your will be done on earth as it is in heaven.

O God, you have charged us to seek your kingdom first, and to love you with all our hearts and minds, and our neighbors as ourselves:

Your will be done on earth as it is in heaven.

From all unwillingness to learn your will, from clinging to our own plans and desires, from all want of faith in your purpose:

Save us, O God.

From refusal to follow your will for us when we see it, from blinding ourselves to your call by our own ambitions, from the shame of turning back when once we have set out in the way of discipleship:

Save us, O God.

O Lord Jesus Christ, who by your delight in doing your Father's will, and by your faithfulness to it even unto death, has left us an example that we should follow in your steps:

Give us grace to follow courageously and faithfully where you have led the way, for your Name's sake.

A Litany for Christian Unity

(The following is based on a prayer written by Abbe Paul Couturier of France, a Roman Catholic, for use during the Week of Prayer for Christian Unity.)

For our controversies often full of ironies, of narrowness of spirit, and of exaggeration with regard to non-Christian people, for our intransigencies and for our severe judgments:

Forgive us, Lord.

For the culpable violence which has been exercised in history among Christians:

Forgive us, Lord.

For the proud or complacent attitudes which we have manifested through the centuries toward other Christians, and for our lack of comprehension of the good that is in them:

Forgive us, Lord.

Above linguistic, racial, national frontiers, unite us, Jesus. Above our ignorance, our prejudices, our instinctive enmities:

Unite us, Jesus.

O God, so that there may be one fold and one Shepherd:

Gather dispersed Christians.

O God, in order that peace may at last reign in the world:

Gather dispersed Christians.

O God, for the greatest joy in the heart of your Son:

Gather dispersed Christians.

Meditations

O God of unchangeable power and eternal light: Look favorably on your whole Church, that wonderful and sacred mystery; by the effectual working of your providence, carry out in tranquility the plan of salvation; let the whole world see and know that things which were cast down are being raised up, and things which had grown old are being made new, and that all things are being brought to their perfection by him through whom all things were made, your Son Jesus Christ our Lord.

🔱

Who shall separate us from the love of Christ? Shall tribulation, or distress, or persecution, or famine, or nakedness, or peril, or sword? No, in all these things we are more than conquerors through him who loved us. For I am sure that neither death, nor life, nor angels, nor principalities, nor things present, nor things to come, nor powers, nor height, nor depth, nor anything else in all creation, will be able to separate us from the love of God in Christ Jesus our Lord.

—*Romans 8:35, 37-39*

There is a really deep well inside me. And in it dwells God. Sometimes I am there too. But more often stones and grit block the well, and God is buried beneath. Then he must be dug out again.

One ought to be able to live without books, without anything. There will always be a small patch of sky above, and there will always be enough space to fold two hands in prayer. For once you have begun to walk with God, you need only keep on walking with him and all of life becomes one long stroll.

From Etty: The Letters and Diaries of Etty Hillesum, 1941-1943, *written during the Nazi occupation of the Netherlands. Hillesum was killed at Auschwitz.*

For the Lenten Season

Blessed Lord, help me to go into the wilderness of quiet and meditation with you during these forty days. Give me grace to examine myself honestly, and to put away everything that keeps me from following you faithfully.

Almighty God, who has said that we shall not live by bread alone but by you, enable me to still all earthly desires and to long only for those things which truly satisfy the soul.

O Holy Spirit, by whose aid alone we can be masters of ourselves, abide in me and give me self-control. Strengthen me to keep my tongue from angry and unkind words, and my body always as a temple suitable for you.

Heavenly Father, whose Blessed Son taught us to be perfect in love as you are, help me to love my neighbor as myself. May the compassionate heart of Jesus ever be my inspiration and example, that your love may be glorified by mine.

Lord Jesus, who commanded your disciples to take up the cross and follow you, let me not falter in my self-denial before this stern discipline. Whatever sacrifice you would have me make for you, give me grace to make it with a willing and joyful heart.

For Holy Week

Almighty God, our heavenly Father, grant to us now, as we follow our blessed Lord through the days of his passion, a mind and a will to follow him faithfully all our days.

Blessed Savior, as I follow you through these holy days of your passion—the betrayal, the agony in the garden, the trials and mocking and scourging, and the dread hours upon the cross—quicken in me the spirit of sincere repentance for all my sins and a will to love and serve you all the days of my life.

Jesus said: The Son of Man came not to be served but to serve, and to give his life a ransom for many.

—*Matthew 20:28*

Jesus entered the temple and drove out all who were selling and buying…and he overturned the tables of the money changers and the seats of those who sold doves. He said to them, "It is written, 'My house shall be called a house of prayer,' but you are making it a den of robbers."

—*Matthew 21:12-13*

He left them, went out of the city to Bethany, and spent the night there.

—*Matthew 21:17*

The disciples did as Jesus had directed them, and they prepared the Passover meal.

—*Matthew 26:19*

And during supper Jesus, knowing that the Father had given all things into his hands, and that he had come from God and was going to God, got up from the table, took off his outer robe, and tied a towel around himself. Then he poured water into a basin and began to wash the disciples' feet and to wipe them with the towel that was tied around him.

—*John 13:3-5*

While they were eating, Jesus took a loaf of bread, and after blessing it he broke it, gave it to the disciples, and said, "Take, eat; this is my body." Then he took a cup, and after giving thanks he gave it to them saying, "Drink from it, all of you; for this is my blood of the covenant, which is poured out for many for the forgiveness of sins."

—*Matthew 26:26-28*

They went to a place called Gethsemane; and he said to his disciples, "Sit here while I pray." He took with him Peter and James and John, and began to be distressed and agitated. And he said to them, "I am deeply grieved, even to death; remain here, and keep awake." And going a little farther, he threw himself on the ground and prayed that, if it were possible, the hour might pass from him. He said, "Abba, Father, for you all things are possible; remove this cup from me; yet, not what I want, but what you want."

—*Mark 14:32-36*

When they came to the place that is called Golgotha (the Skull), they crucified Jesus there with the criminals, one on his right and one on his left. Then Jesus said, "Father, forgive them; for they do not know what they are doing."

—Luke 23:33-34

⚜

When it was noon, darkness came over the whole land until three in the afternoon. At three o'clock Jesus cried out with a loud voice, "Eloi, Eloi, lema sabachthani?" which means, "My God, my God, why have you forsaken me?"

—Mark 15:33-34

⚜

Then Jesus, crying with a loud voice, said, "Father, into your hands I commend my spirit." Having said this, he breathed his last.

—Luke 23:46

Lord, have mercy upon us.
Christ, have mercy upon us.
Lord, have mercy upon us.

Blessed Savior:

By your entry into Jerusalem:

Give us courage to accept the duties and responsibilities of our faith.

By your cleansing of the Temple:

Give us zeal for righteousness and for your holy church.

By your washing of the disciples' feet:

Take away our pride, and endue us with the spirit of true humility.

By your breaking of the bread and giving of the cup:

Help us give ourselves for the life of the world.

By your acceptance in the garden of the will of God:

Help us seek to learn the will of God, and to surrender our own will to it.

By your forgiveness of those who nailed you to the cross:

Make us ready to forgive.

By your faithfulness unto death, even the death of the cross:

Make us steadfast in our faith to our life's end, for your Name's sake.

⚜

Almighty and everliving God, in your tender love for the human race you sent your Son our Savior Jesus Christ to take upon him our nature, and to suffer death upon the cross, giving us the example of his great humility: Mercifully grant that we may walk in his way of suffering, and also share in his resurrection.

Benedictions

Unto God's gracious mercy and protection we commit you. The Lord bless you and keep you. The Lord make his face to shine upon you and be gracious unto you. The Lord lift up the light of his countenance upon you, and give you peace, both now and for evermore.

Peace be with you all that are in Christ Jesus.

May the true God of all things, who sent forth the Holy Spirit upon the apostles in Jerusalem on the day of Pentecost, send the Spirit now upon you, to guard you and impart to you his bounty, that the fruits of the Spirit—love, joy, peace, patience, kindness, generosity, faithfulness, gentleness, and self-control—may be yours, this day and forever. Amen.

—*adapted from Cyril of Jerusalem*

May the strength of God pilot us.
May the power of God preserve us.
May the wisdom of God instruct us.
May the hand of God protect us.
May the way of God direct us.
May the shield of God defend us.

—adapted from St. Patrick

🔱

Now to him who by the power at work within us is able to accomplish abundantly more than we can ask or imagine, to him be glory in the church and in Christ Jesus to all generations, forever and ever.

🔱

Go forth into the world in peace; be of good courage; hold fast that which is good; render to no one evil for evil; strengthen the fainthearted; support the weak; help the afflicted; honor all people. Love and serve the Lord, rejoicing in the power of the Holy Spirit. And the blessing of God Almighty, the Father, the Son, and the Holy Spirit be upon you and remain with you for ever.

Index

Index

Prayers for All Occasions

Index

Prayers for All Occasions